DRINKING ANIMALS COLORING BOOK FOR ADULTS RELAXATION

This book belongs to:

____

WHISKEY MANHATTAN COCKTAIL
Preparation time: 15 min
Serves: 1
Ingredients:
- Ice, as required
- 1½ fluid ounces bourbon whiskey
- ½ fluid ounce sweet vermouth
- 1 dash bitters
- 1 maraschino cherry
Instructions:
1. Fill a martini shaker with ice and place the whiskey, vermouth and bitters.
2. Shake vigorously for about 30 seconds.
3. Transfer into 2 chilled cocktail glasses and garnish each with a cherry.
4 Serve immediately.

ESPRESSO
WHISKEY
COCKTAIL
Ingredients:
- Ice cubes, as required
- 4 ounces espresso, room t°
- 2 ounces rye whiskey
- ½ ounce simple syrup
- 2 dashes of bitters
- 2 (1-inch) piece lemon peel
Instructions:
1. Fill a cocktail shaker with ice and place the espresso, bourbon, simple syrup.
2. Cover and shake vigorously for about 30 seconds.
3. Through a strainer, strain into ice filled glasses.
4. Twist 1 lemon peel over each cocktail and serve.
Preparation time: 15 min
Serves: 2

WHITE WINE SPRITZER
Ingredients:
-6 ounces chilled white wine
- 2 ounces cold club soda
- Ice cubes, as required
- 2 lemon slices
Preparation time: 15 min
Serves: 2
Instructions:
1. Fill 2 glasses with ice and top with the wine, followed by the soda.
2. Garnish each glass with a lemon slice and serve.

CHAMPAGNE & RUM COCKTAIL
Preparation time: 15 min
Serves: 1
Ingredients:
- 2/3 fluid ounce Blue Curacao
- 2/3 fluid ounce lemon rum
- 6 fluid ounces champagne
Instructions:
1. In a champagne flute, place the blue curacao and lemon rum.
2. Top with the champagne and serve.

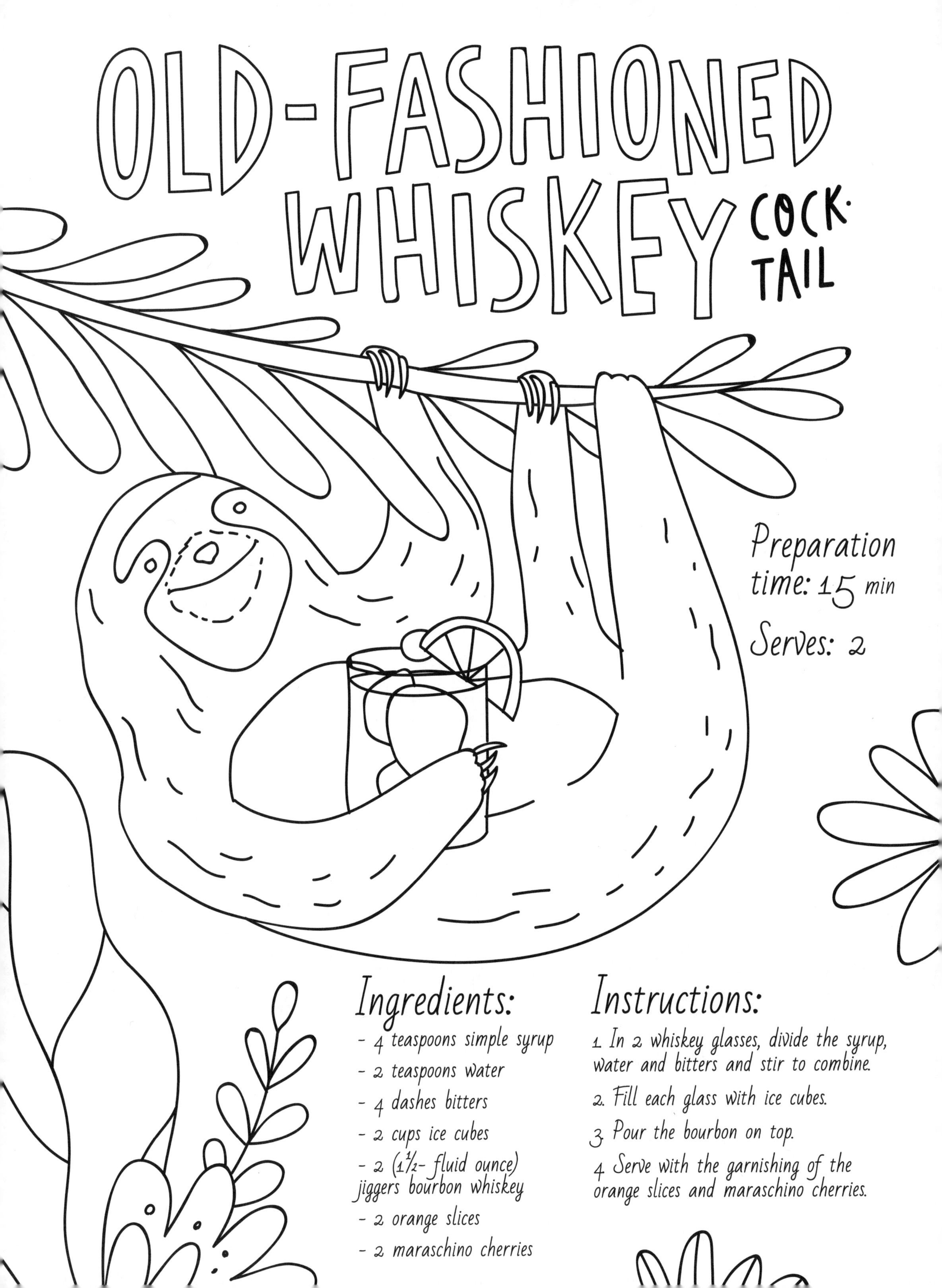
OLD-FASHIONED WHISKEY COCK-TAIL
Preparation time: 15 min
Serves: 2
Ingredients:
- 4 teaspoons simple syrup
- 2 teaspoons water
- 4 dashes bitters
- 2 cups ice cubes
- 2 (1½- fluid ounce) jiggers bourbon whiskey
- 2 orange slices
- 2 maraschino cherries
Instructions:
1 In 2 whiskey glasses, divide the syrup, water and bitters and stir to combine.
2. Fill each glass with ice cubes.
3 Pour the bourbon on top.
4 Serve with the garnishing of the orange slices and maraschino cherries.

CHAMPAGNE PUNCH COCKTAIL
Ingredients:
- 3 cups chilled cranberry juice
- 3 cups chilled champagne
- ¼ cup orange liqueur
- 2 cups frozen cranberries
- ½ orange, cut into slices
Instructions:
1. In a punch bowl, add the cranberry juice, champagne and orange liqueur and stir to combine.
2. Add the cranberries, orange slices and enjoy!
Preparation time: 15 min
Serves: 10

MINT JULEP
Preparation time: 15 min
Serves: 2
Ingredients:
- 20 fresh mint leaves
- 2 teaspoons white sugar
- 2 tablespoons warm water
- 1 cup ice, crushed
- 4 fluid ounces cognac
- 4 fluid ounces chilled dry sparkling wine
Instructions:
1. In 2 tall cocktail glasses, divide the mint, sugar and water and with the back of a spoon, crush to release extracts.
2. Fill the glasses with ice.
3. Add the cognac and stir to combine.
4. Top with the wine and serve.

BEER & VODKA
COCKTAIL
Preparation time: 10 min
Serves: 10
Ingredients:
- 4 (12 fluid ounce) cans light beer
- 2 (12 ounce) cans frozen lemonade concentrate
- 12 fluid ounces vodka
Instructions:
1. In a pitcher, add the beer and lemonade and stir to combine.
2. Add the vodka and stir to combine.
3. Serve immediately.

CHERRY BEER
Preparation time: 5 min
Serves: 2
Ingredients:
- 1½ cup cherry juice
- 2 (12 fluid ounce) cans wheat beer
Instructions:
1. Divide cherry juice into 2 glasses and top with the beer.
2. Serve immediately.

BEER MARGARITA
Preparation time: 10 min
Serves: 6
Ingredients:
- 3 (12 fluid ounce) cans beer
1 (12 fluid ounce) can limeade concentrate
- 1½ cups gold tequila
- Ice cubes
- 1 whole lime, cut into 6 wedges
Instructions:
1. In a large pitcher, add the beer, limeade and tequila and stir to combine.
2. Fill tall serving glasses with ice cubes and top with the beer mixture.
3. Squeeze 1 lime wedge into each glass and serve.

GIN MARTINI COCKTAIL
Preparation time: 15 min
Serves: 1
Instructions:
1. In a martini shaker, add the ice cubes, gin and vermouth.
2. Cover and shake for at least 30 seconds.
3. Through a strainer, strain into a chilled cocktail glass.
4. Garnish with olives and serve.
Ingredients:
- Ice cubes
- 2½ ounces gin
- ½ ounce dry vermouth
- 3 olives

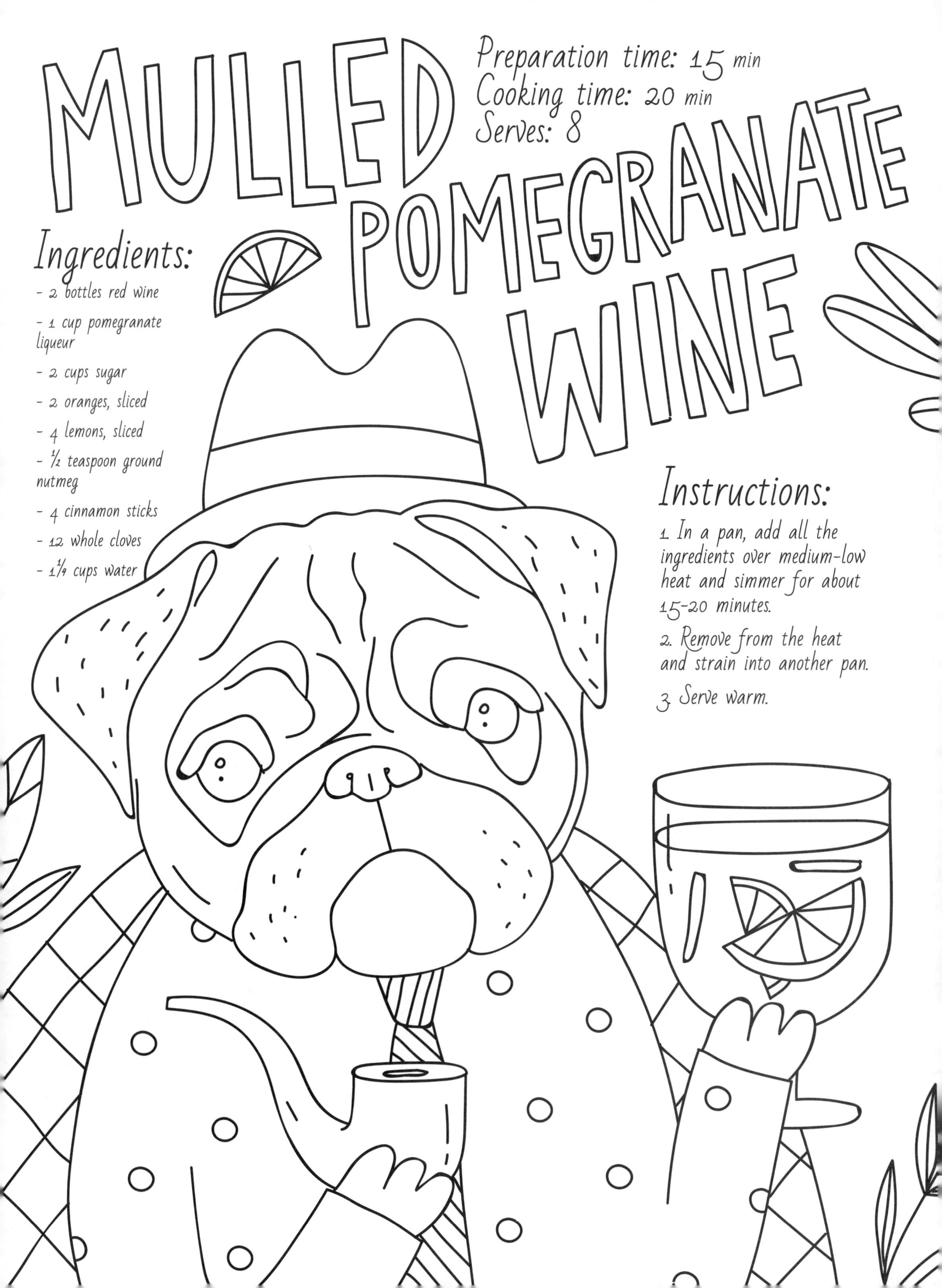
MULLED POMEGRANATE WINE
Preparation time: 15 min
Cooking time: 20 min
Serves: 8
Ingredients:
- 2 bottles red wine
- 1 cup pomegranate liqueur
- 2 cups sugar
- 2 oranges, sliced
- 4 lemons, sliced
- ½ teaspoon ground nutmeg
- 4 cinnamon sticks
- 12 whole cloves
- 1¼ cups water
Instructions:
1. In a pan, add all the ingredients over medium-low heat and simmer for about 15-20 minutes.
2. Remove from the heat and strain into another pan.
3. Serve warm.

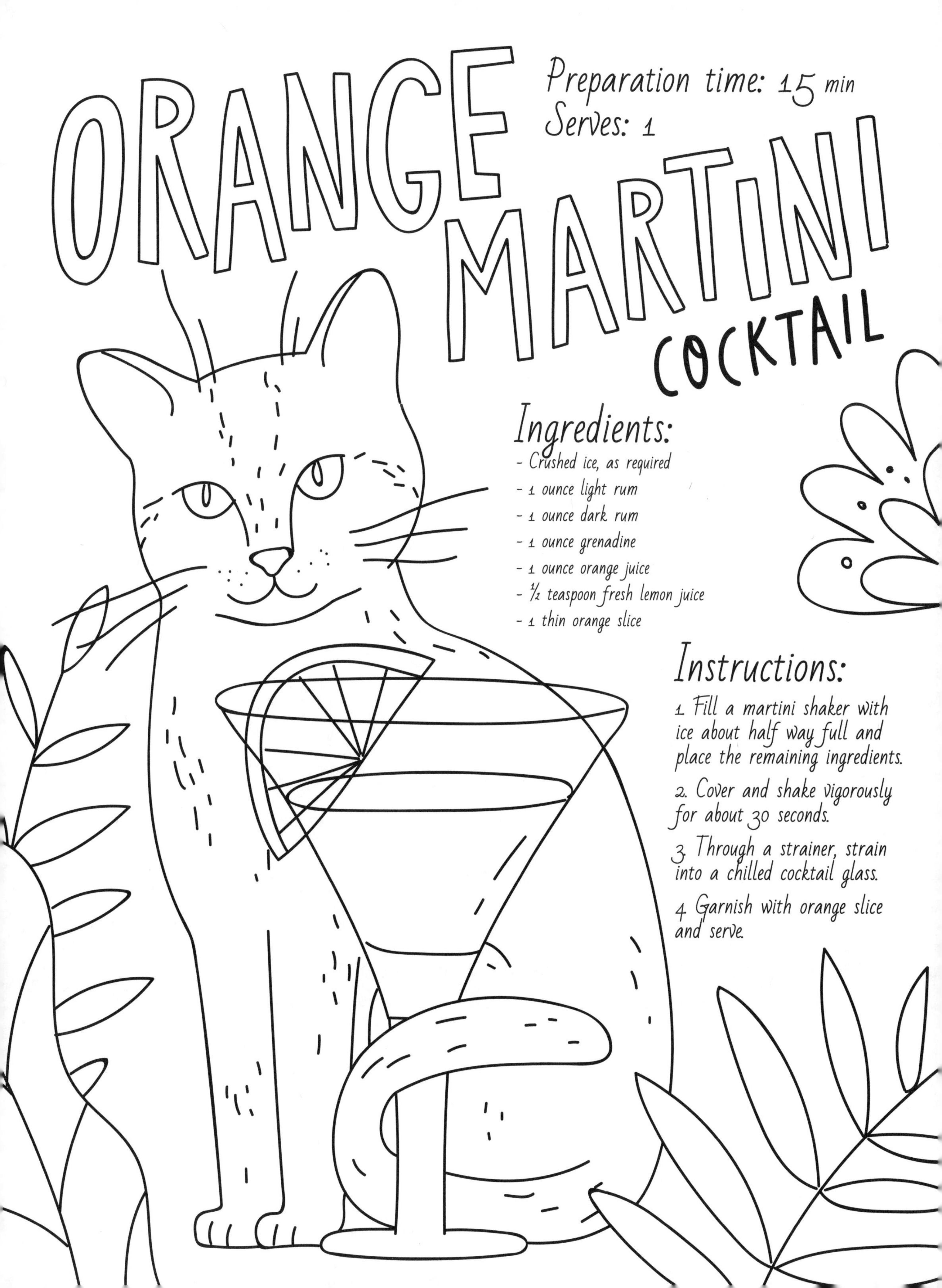
ORANGE
MARTINI
COCKTAIL
Preparation time: 15 min
Serves: 1
Ingredients:
- Crushed ice, as required
- 1 ounce light rum
- 1 ounce dark rum
- 1 ounce grenadine
- 1 ounce orange juice
- ½ teaspoon fresh lemon juice
- 1 thin orange slice
Instructions:
1. Fill a martini shaker with ice about half way full and place the remaining ingredients.
2. Cover and shake vigorously for about 30 seconds.
3. Through a strainer, strain into a chilled cocktail glass.
4 Garnish with orange slice and serve.

CHOCOLATE
COCKTAIL
MARTINI
Preparation time: 15 min
Serves: 1
Ingredients:
- 2 fluid ounces chocolate vodka
- ½ fluid ounce chocolate liqueur
- ¼ fluid ounce coffee flavored liqueur
- ¼ fluid ounce cinnamon schnapps
- Chopped chocolate, for garnishing
Instructions:
1. Fill a martini shaker with ice about half way full and place the remaining ingredients.
2. Cover and shake vigorously for about 30 seconds.
3. Through a strainer, strain into a chilled cocktail glass.
4. Garnish with chocolate pieces and serve.

Preparation time: 15 min
Serves: 2
MINT MOJITO
Ingredients:
- 4 teaspoons white sugar
- fresh mint leaves
- 1 lime, cut into 6 wedges
- 2 (1½ fluid ounce) jiggers lemon-flavored rum
- Ice cubes, as required
- ½ cup carbonated water
Instructions:
1. In 2 serving glass tumblers, divide the sugar and mint leaves and with the back of a spoon, crush vigorously to release extracts.
2. Add 3 lime wedges into each glass and stir vigorously to release some lime juice.
3. Now, divide the rum into glasses and then fill each with ice cubes.
4. Pour the carbonated water on top and stir well.
5. Serve immediately.

HOT IRISH WHISKEY
Preparation time: 15 min
Serves: 2
Ingredients:
- 16 whole cloves
- 2 (¼-inch thick) lemon slices
- 2 tablespoons white sugar
- 1½ cups boiling water
- 2 (1½-fluid ounce) jiggers Irish whiskey
Instructions:
1. Press 8 cloves into the peel of each lemon slice all the way around.
2. Set aside.
3. Divide the sugar into 2 wine glasses.
4. Arrange 1 metal spoon into each glass with the curved side facing upwards.
5. Pour the boiling water over the back of the spoon in each glass and stir until sugar is dissolved.
6. Divide the whiskey into each glass.
7. Add the lemon slice into each glass and steep for about 1 minute before serving.

LIME DAIQUIRI
Preparation time: 10 min
Serves: 2
Ingredients:
- 2 cups ice cubes
- 3 fluid ounces light rum
- 2 fluid ounces triple sec
- 2 fluid ounces lime juice
- 2 teaspoons white sugar
- 2 lime wedges
Instructions:
1. In a blender, add all the ingredients and pulse until smooth.
2. Transfer into serving glasses and serve with the garnishing of lime wedges.

MANGO &
PINEAPPLE
DAIQUIRI
Preparation time: 15 min
Serves: 2
Ingredients:
- 4 (1½-fluid ounce) jiggers mango nectar
- 2 (1½-fluid ounce) jiggers pineapple juice
- 2 (1½-fluid ounce) jiggers triple sec
- 2 (1½-fluid ounce) jiggers rum
- 1 lime, juiced
- 3 cups ice cubes
Instructions:
1. In a blender, add all the ingredients except the ice and pulse until smooth.
2. Add the ice and pulse highest setting until slushy.
3. Transfer into serving glasses and serve.

BANANA DAIQUIRI
Preparation time: 10 min
Serves: 2
Ingredients:
- 1 large banana, sliced
- 3 fluid ounces light rum
- 2 fluid ounce fresh lime juice
- 1 fluid ounce triple sec
- 2 teaspoons white sugar
- 2 cups ice cubes
Instructions:
1. In a blender, add all the ingredients except the ice and pulse until smooth.
2. Add the ice and pulse highest setting until slushy.
3. Transfer into serving glasses and serve.

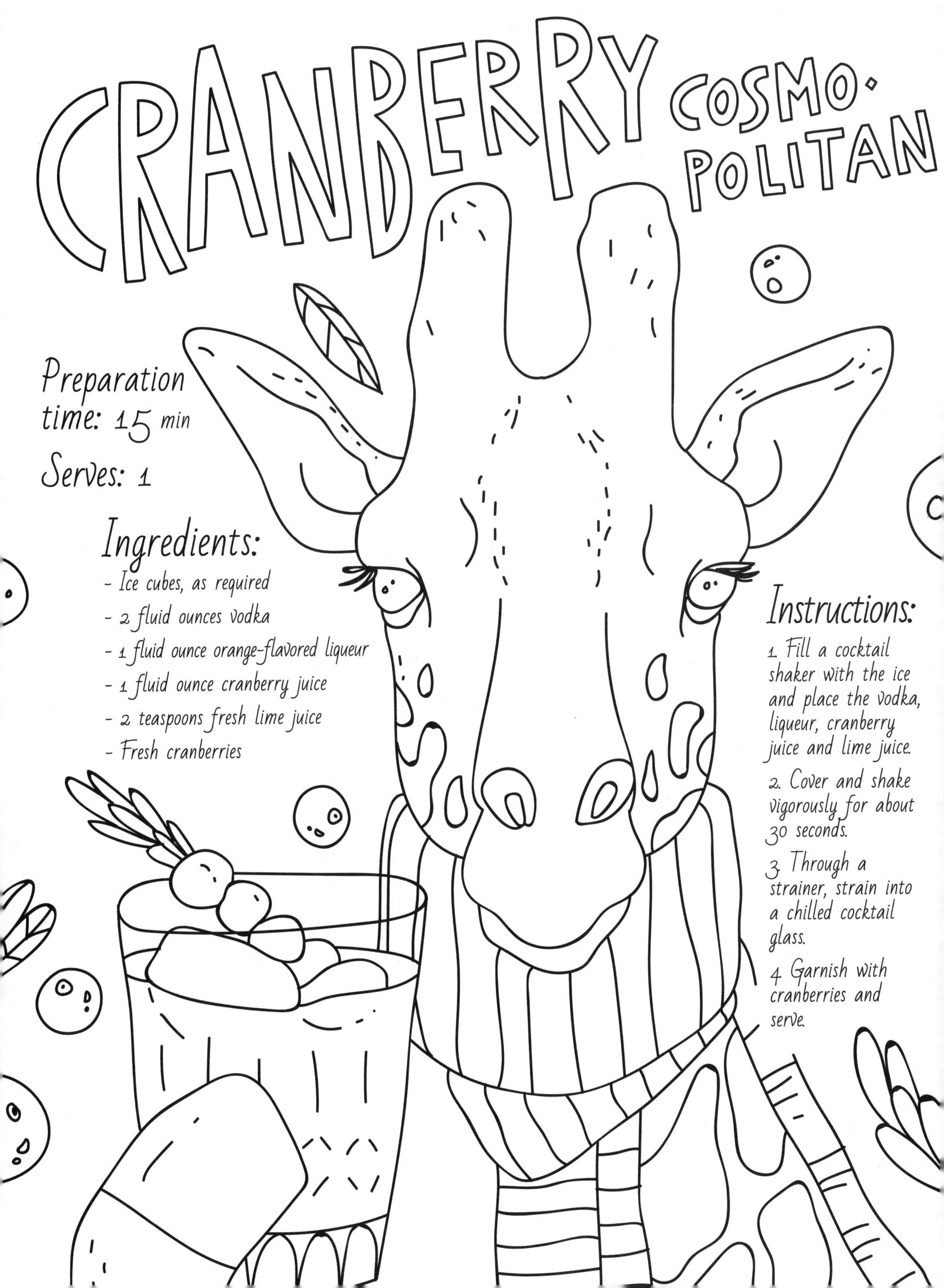
CRANBERRY COSMO-POLITAN
Preparation time: 15 min
Serves: 1
Ingredients:
- Ice cubes, as required
- 2 fluid ounces vodka
- 1 fluid ounce orange-flavored liqueur
- 1 fluid ounce cranberry juice
- 2 teaspoons fresh lime juice
- Fresh cranberries
Instructions:
1. Fill a cocktail shaker with the ice and place the vodka, liqueur, cranberry juice and lime juice.
2. Cover and shake vigorously for about 30 seconds.
3. Through a strainer, strain into a chilled cocktail glass.
4 Garnish with cranberries and serve.

CRANBERRY MOJITO
Ingredients:
- 1 cup fresh mint leaves
- ½ cup sugar
- 1¾ cups light rum
- 1¼ cups fresh lime juice
- 2 (10-ounce) bottles sparkling water, chilled
- ¾ cup frozen cranberry juice cocktail concentrate, thawed
- Ice cubes, as required
Instructions:
1. In a large pitcher, add the mint leaves and sugar and with the back of a spoon, crush vigorously to release extracts.
2. Add the rum and lime juice and stir until sugar is dissolved.
3. Add the sparkling water and cranberry juice concentrate and stir to combine.
4. Fill the glasses with ice and top with the mixture.
5. Serve immediately.
Preparation time: 15 min
Serves: 6

FROZEN COCONUT MOJITO
Preparation time: 15 min
Serves: 2
Ingredients:
- 7 fluid ounces sweetened cream of coconut
- 2½ (1½-fluid ounce) jiggers white rum
- 2½ limes, rind removed
- 5 fresh mint sprigs, leaves removed
- 4 cups ice cubes
- 2 mint sprigs
Instructions:
1. In a blender, add the cream of coconut, rum, limes, mint sprigs and ice and pulse until smooth.
2. Pour into serving glasses and serve with the garnishing of mint sprigs.

WHITE COSMOPOLITAN
Preparation time: 15 min
Serves: 1
Ingredients:
- Ice cubes, as required
- 1½ fluid ounces vodka
- 1 fluid ounce white cranberry juice
- ½ fluid ounce triple sec
- ¼ fluid ounce lime juice
- 1 lime slice
Instructions:
1. Fill a cocktail shaker with the ice and place the remaining ingredients except the lime slice.
2. Cover and shake vigorously for about 30 seconds.
3. Through a strainer, strain into a chilled cocktail glass.
4. Serve with the garnishing of lime slice.

WATERMELON
COSMOPOLITAN
Ingredients:
- 2 cups watermelon, peeled, seeded and cubed
- Ice cubes, as required
- 1 (1½ fluid ounce) jigger vodka
- 1 mint sprig
Preparation time: 15 min
Serves: 1
Instructions:
1 In a blender, add the watermelon and pulse until smooth.
2. Through a fine mesh strainer, strain the pureed watermelon into a bowl, discarding the pulp.
3 Fill a cocktail shaker with the ice and place the vodka and watermelon juice.
4 Cover and shake vigorously for about 30 seconds.
5 Through a strainer, strain into a chilled cocktail glass.
6 Serve with the garnishing of mint sprig.